Antique Bird Art V
for Adult Colorists
By Carol Mennig

25 Antique Bird Print Designs
By Francis Orpen Morris
(1810-1893)

BEE EATER

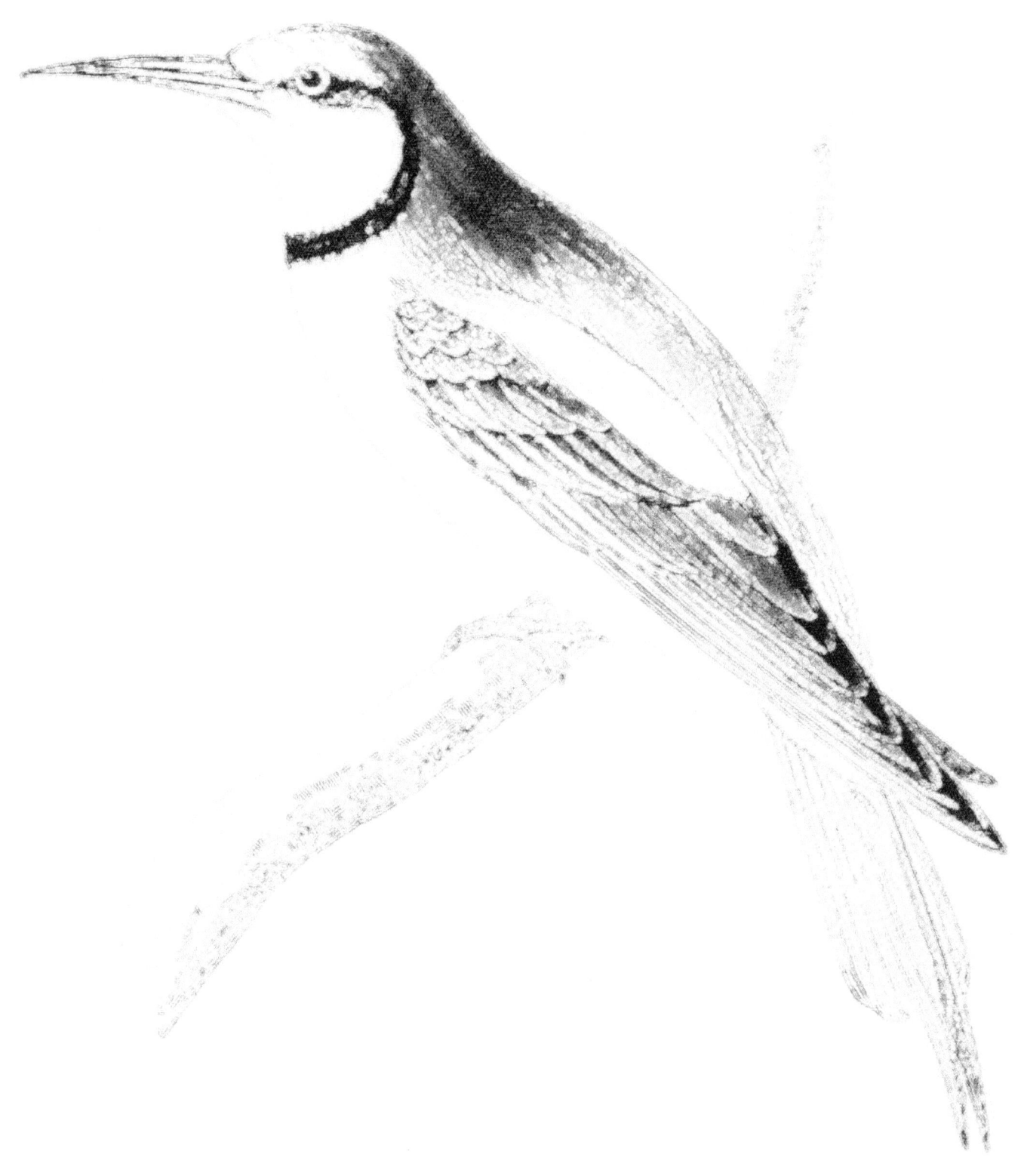

BELTED KINGFISHER

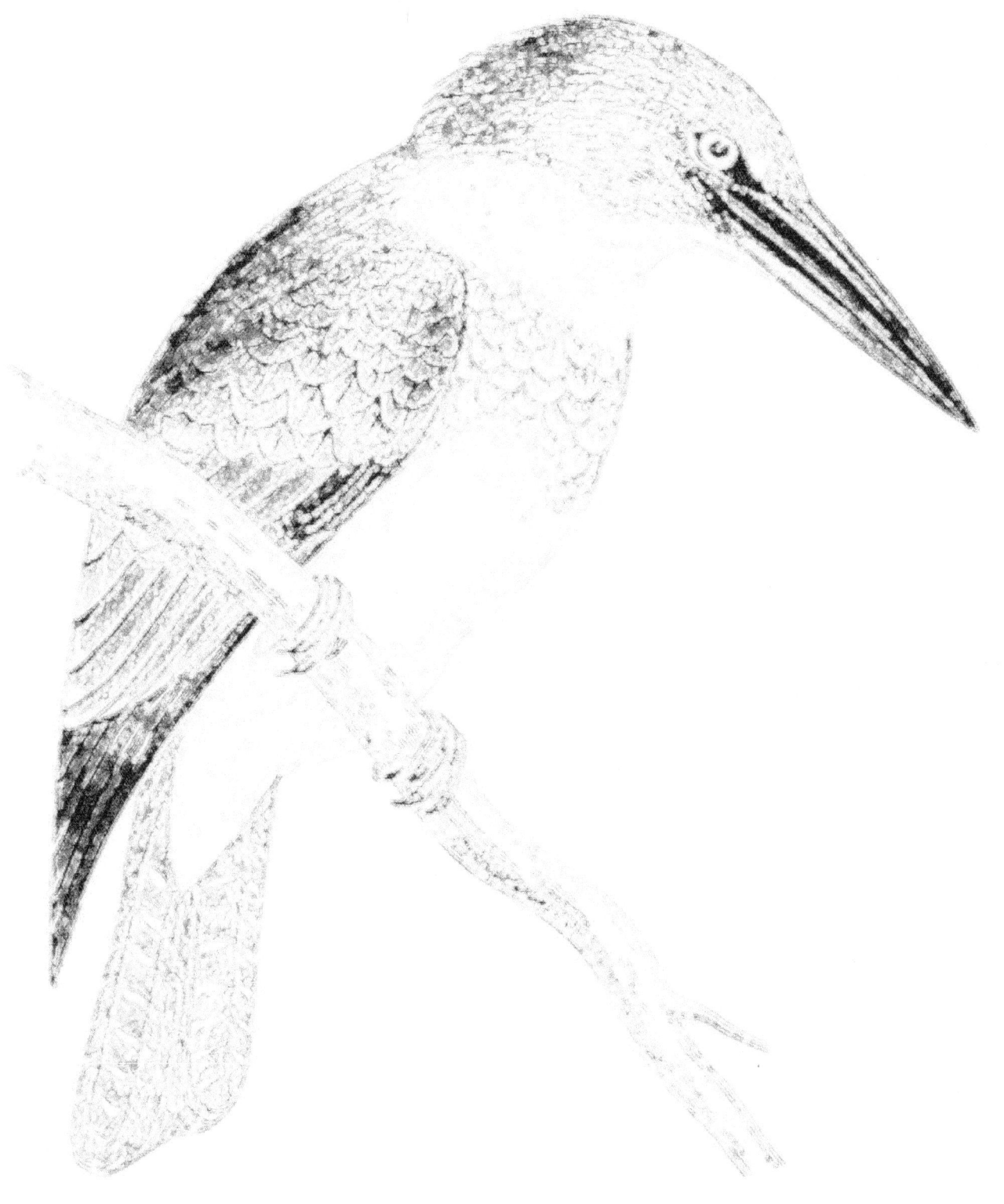

BITTERN

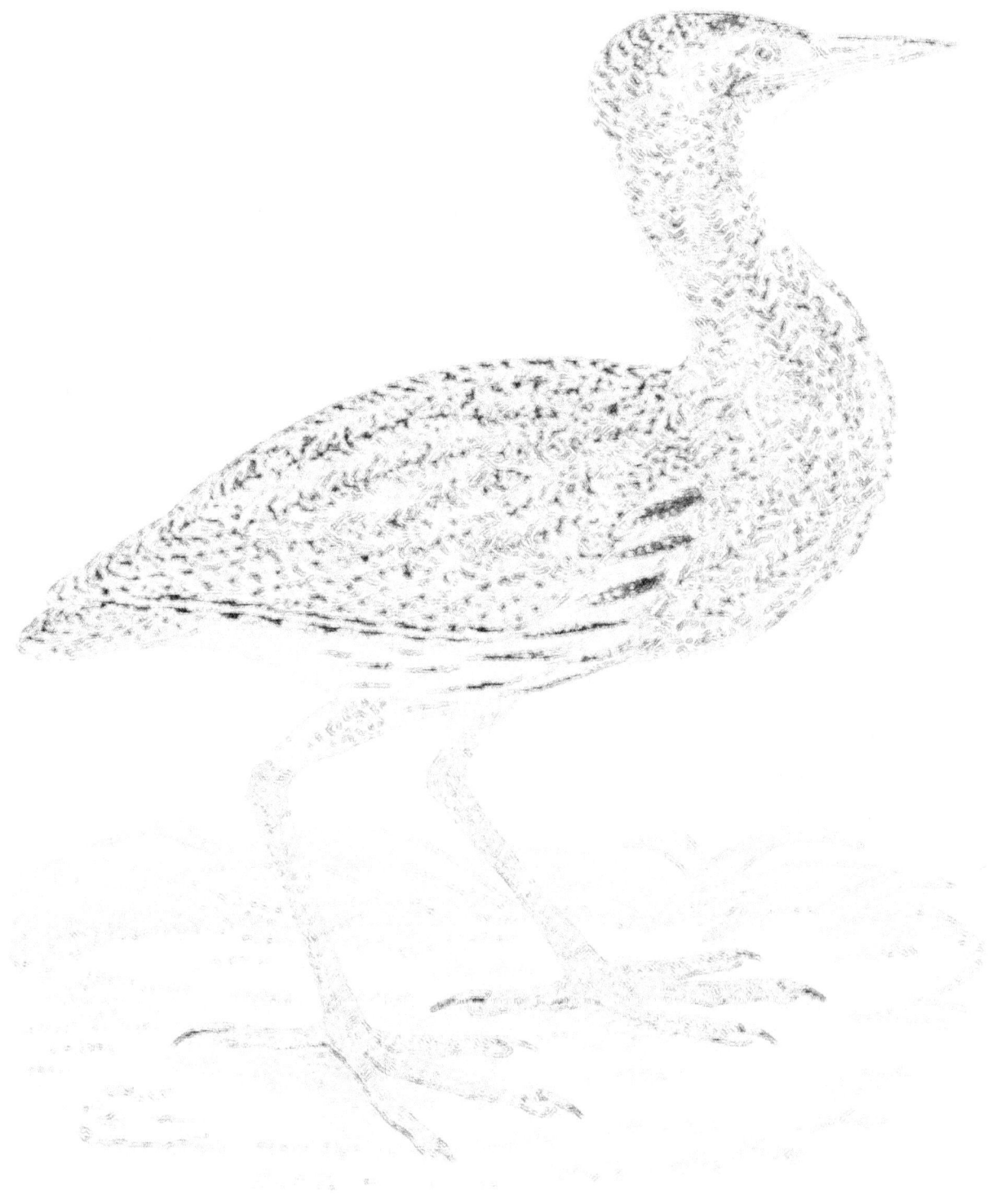

BLACK KITE

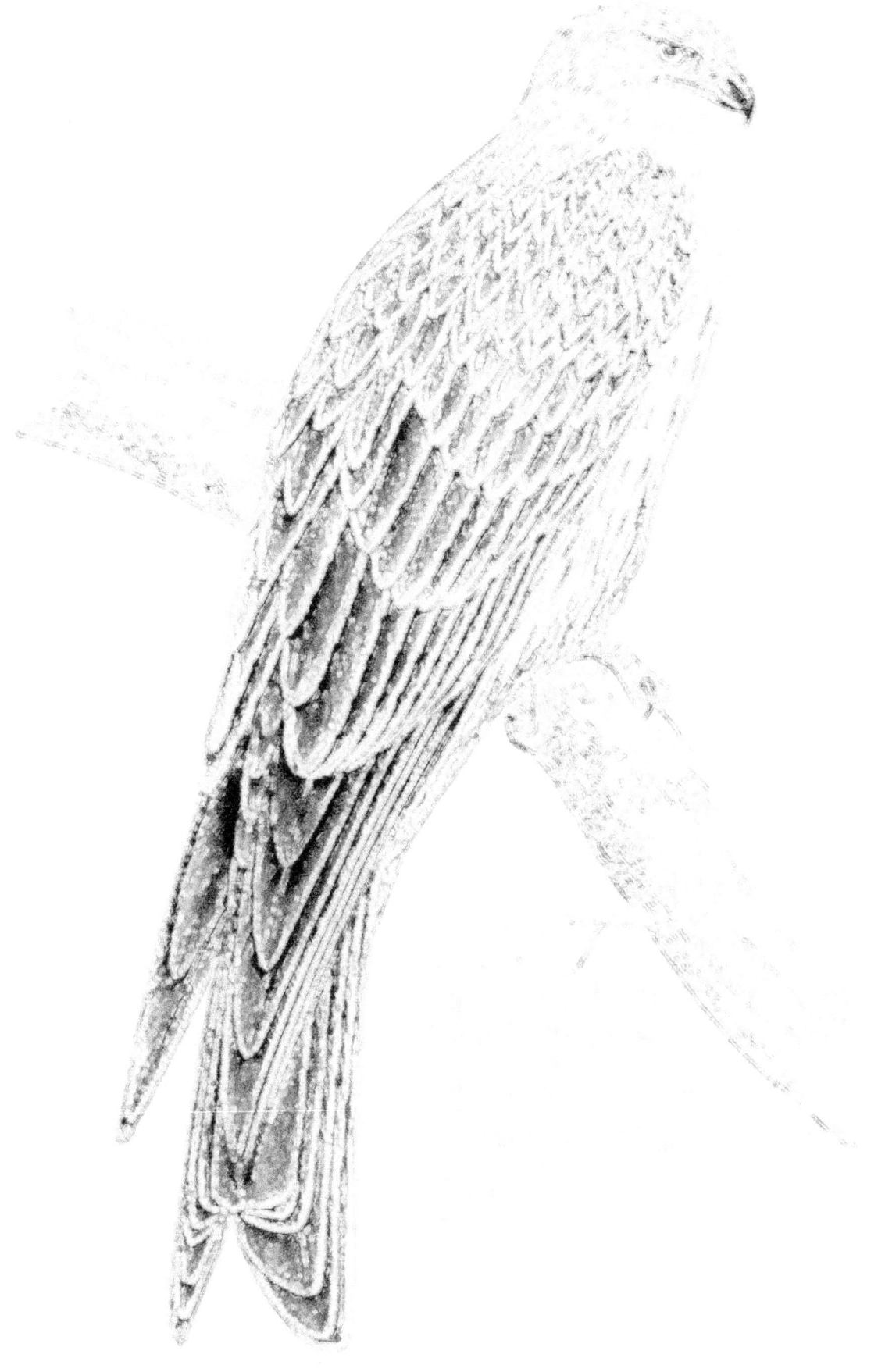

BLACK STORK

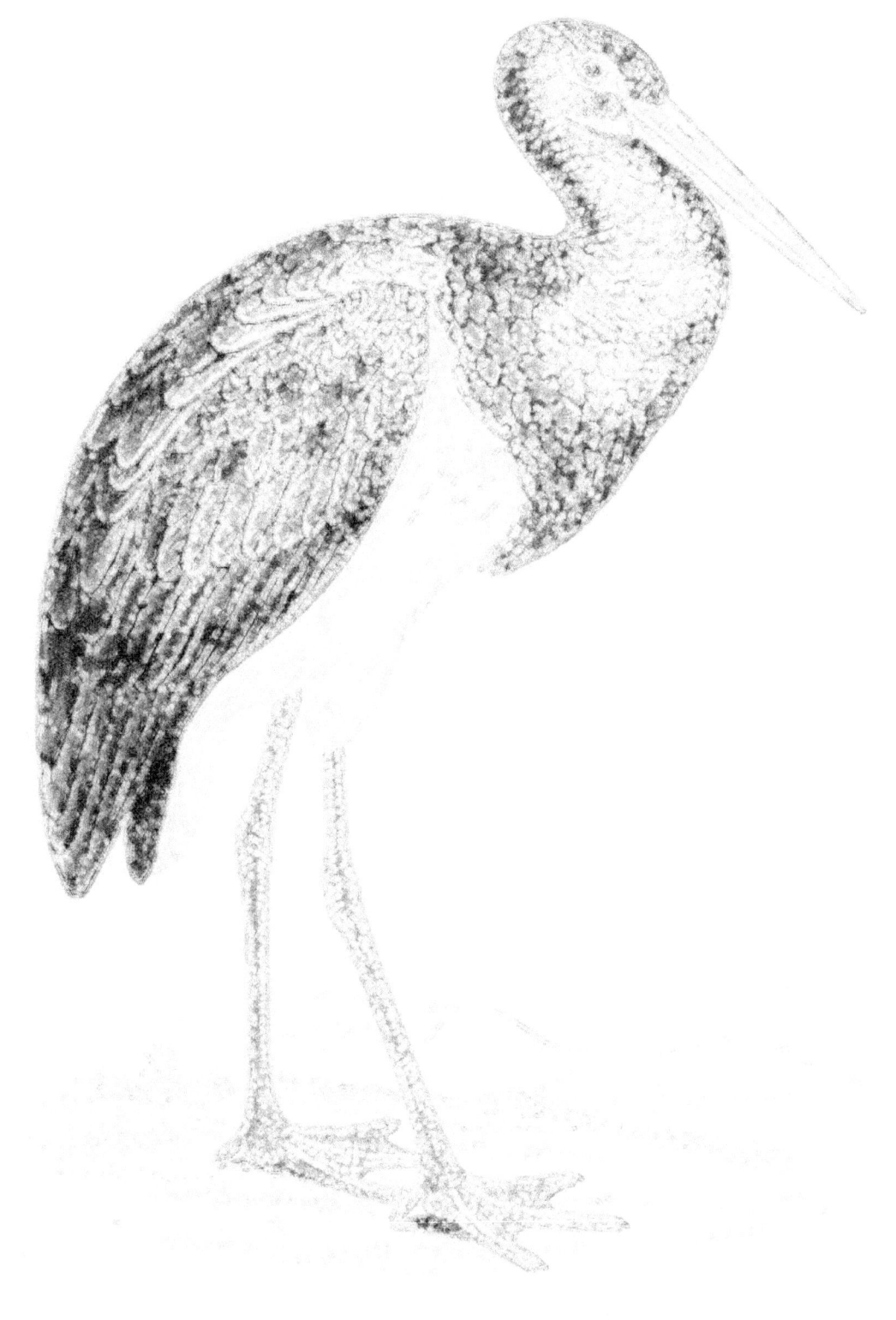

BLACK-TAILED GODWIT

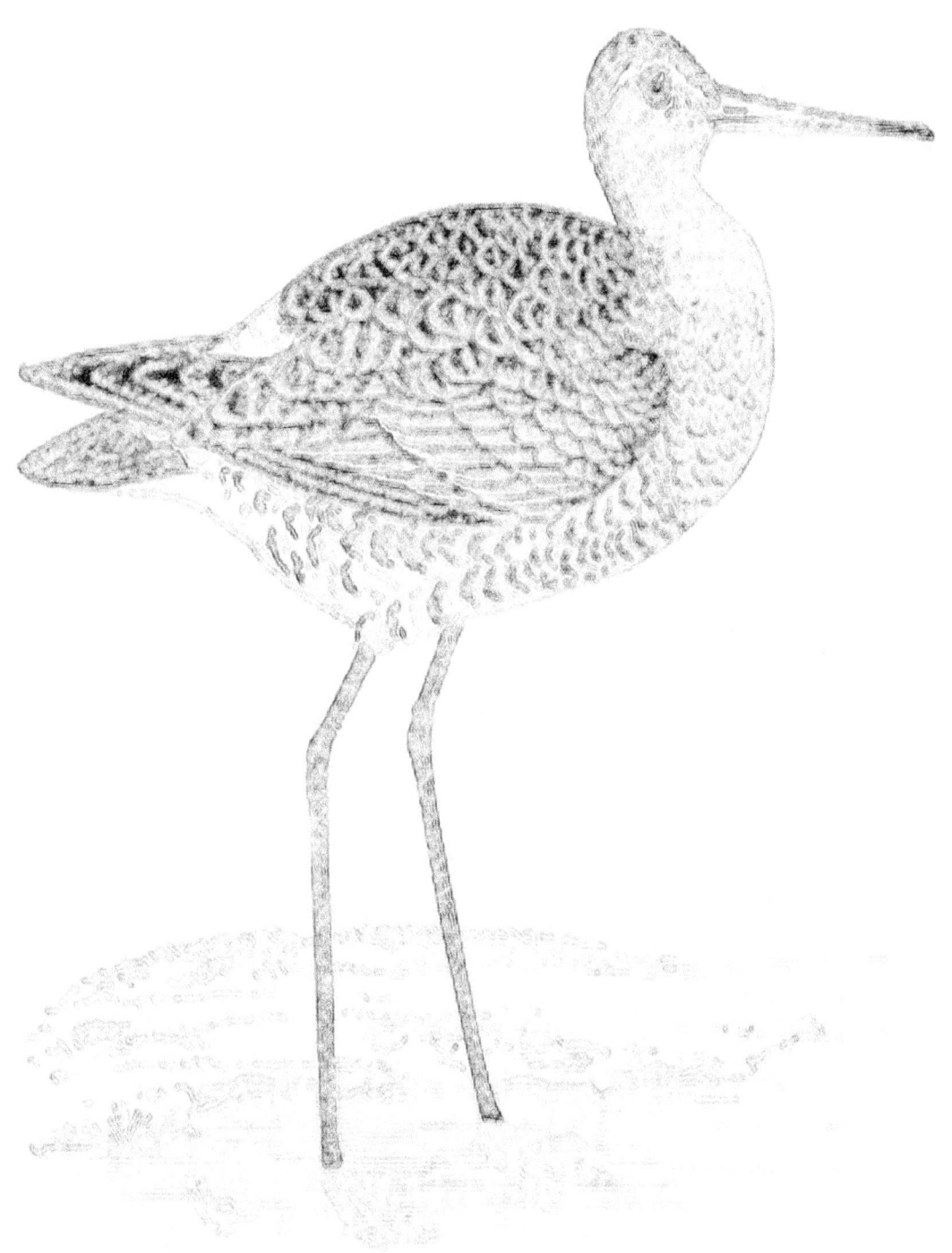

BLACK-HEADED BUNTING

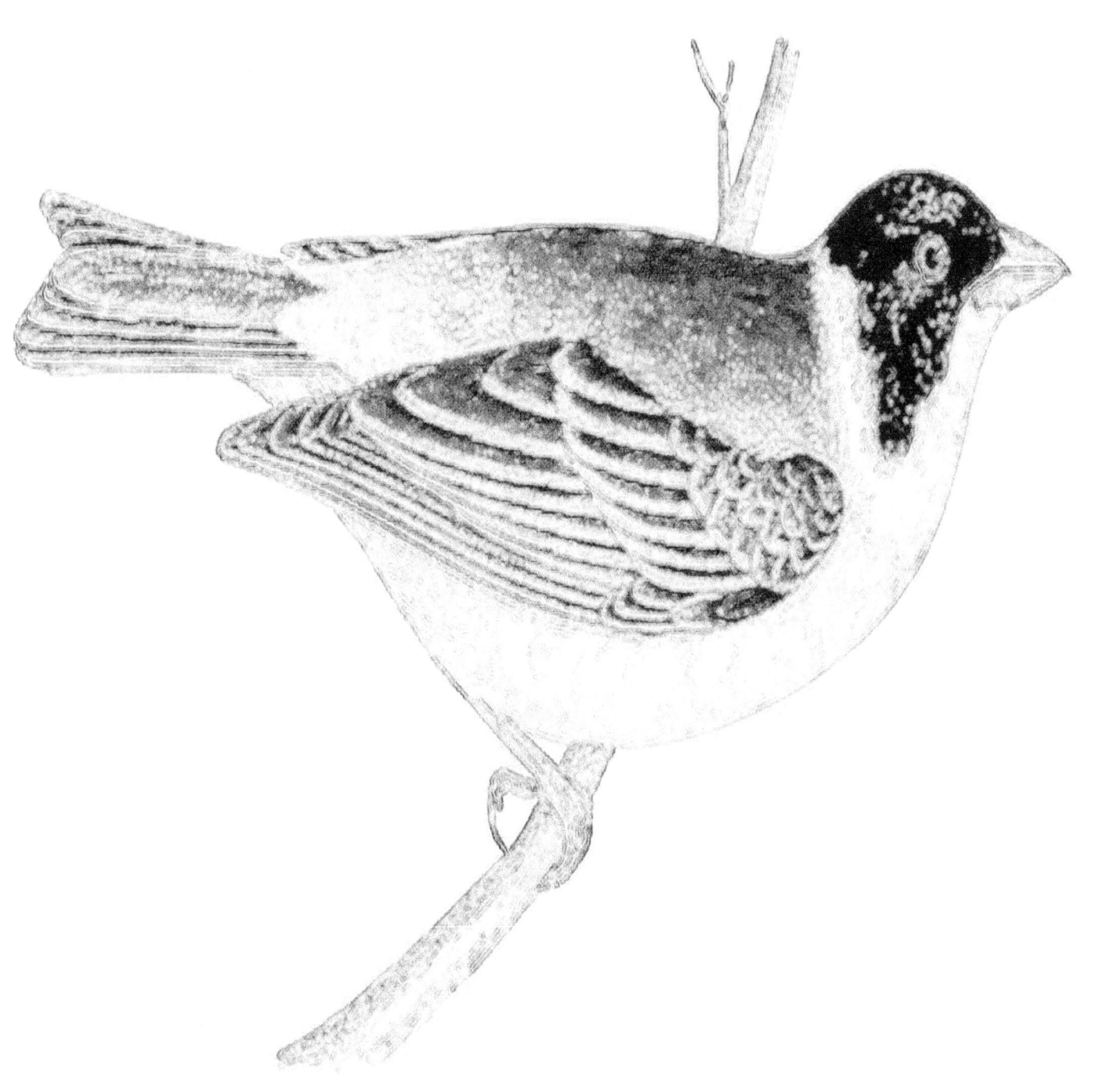

BLACKSTART

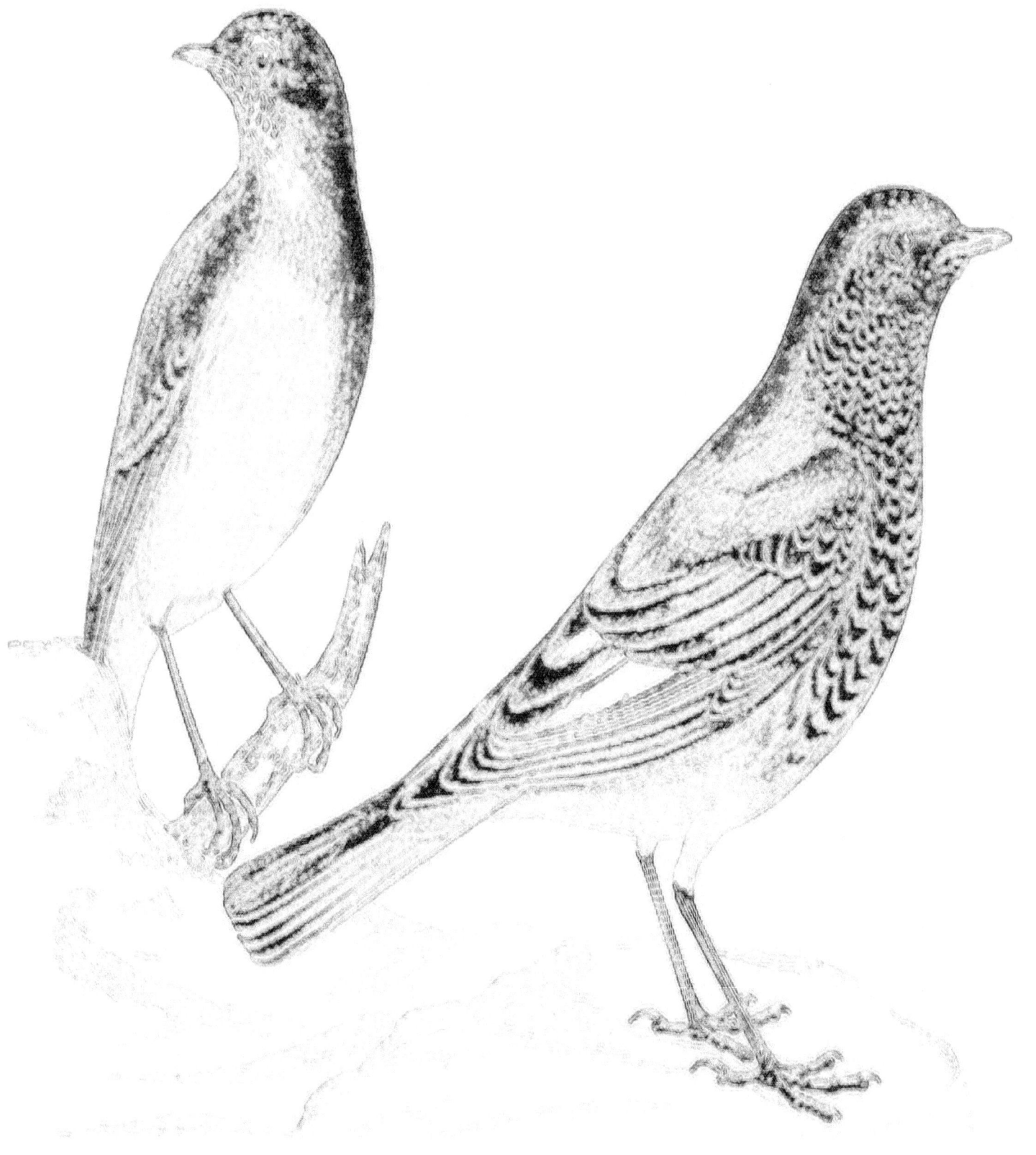

BLACK-THROADED WHEATEAR

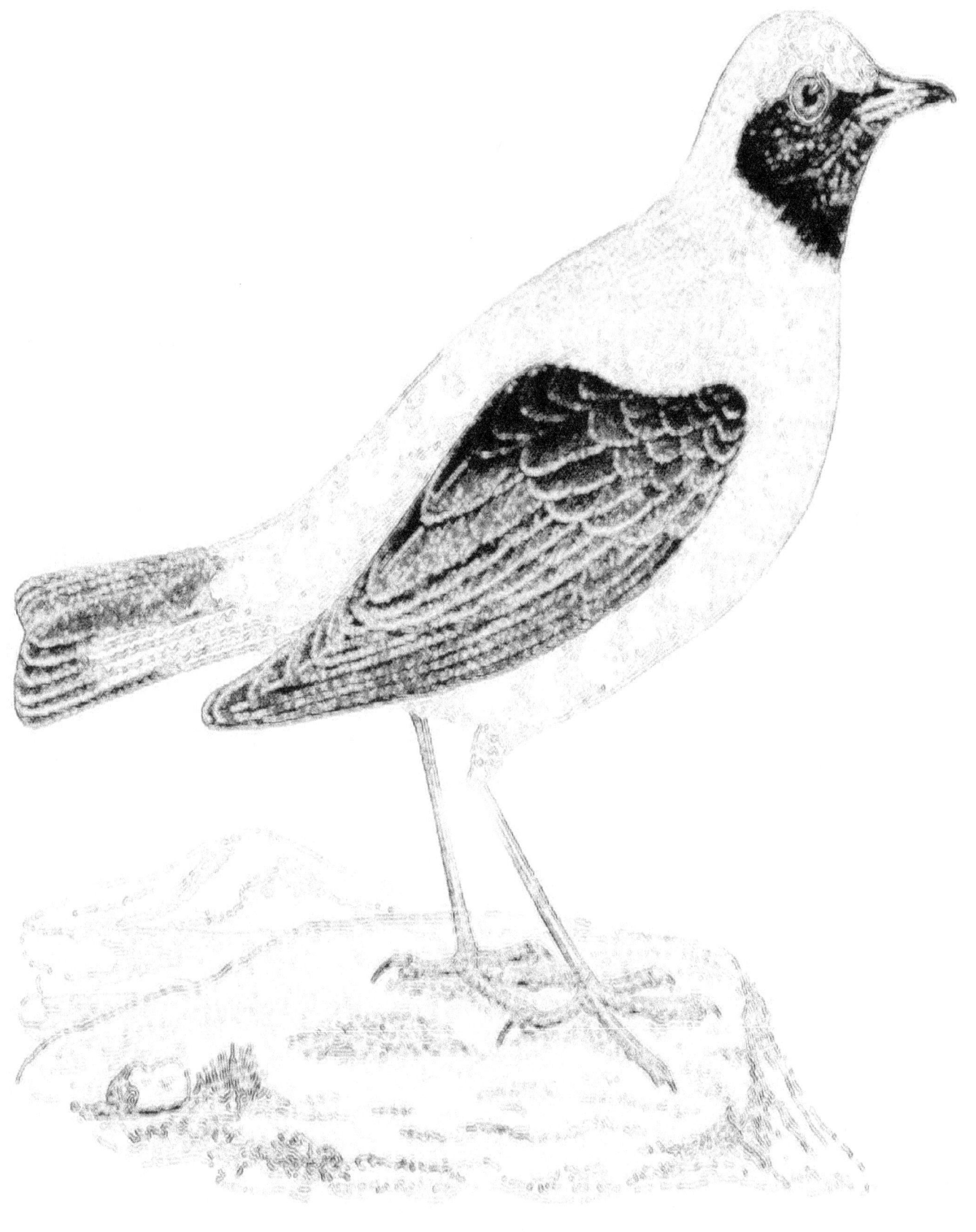

BLUEBREAST

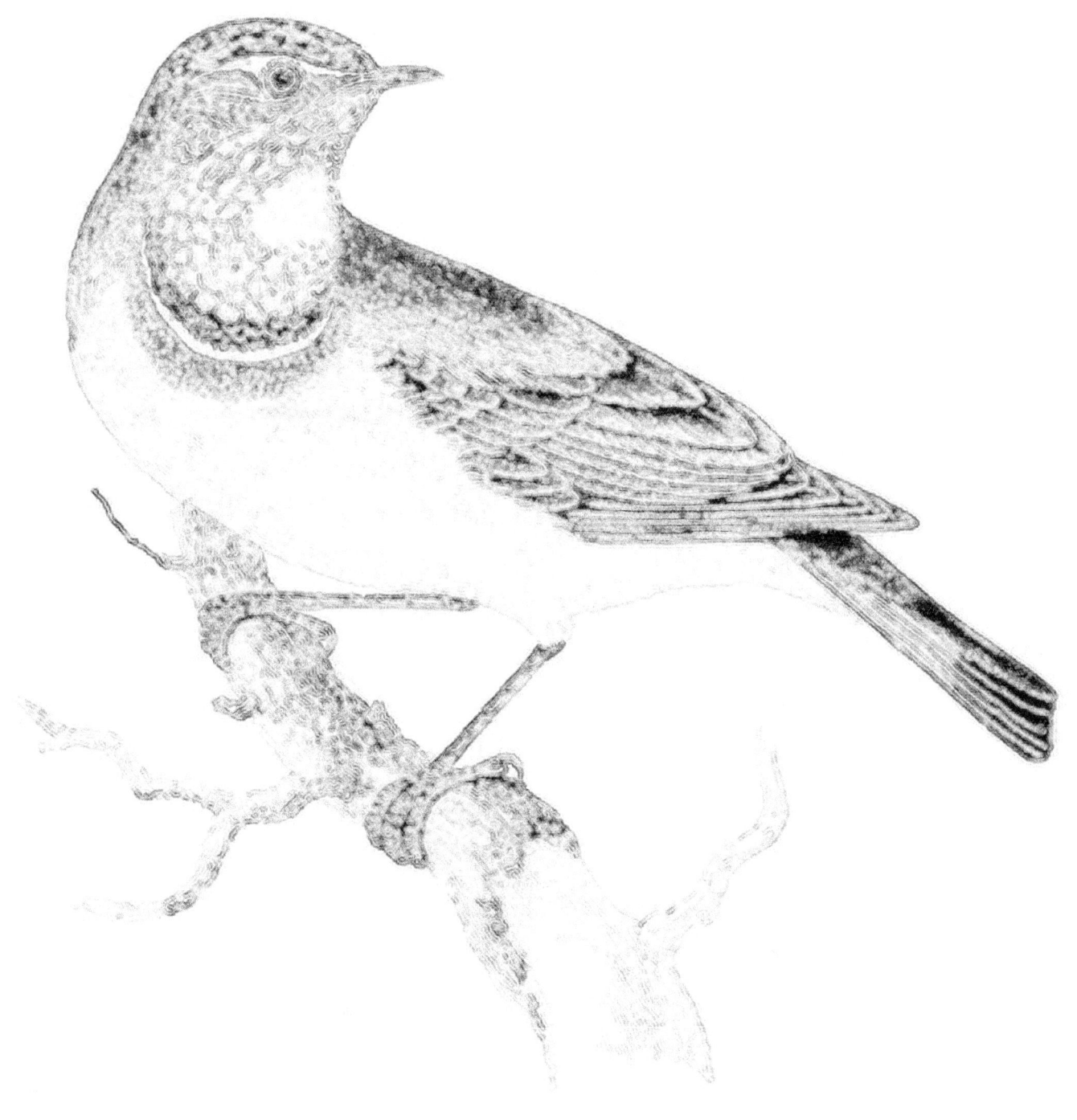

BROAD-BILLED SANDPIPER

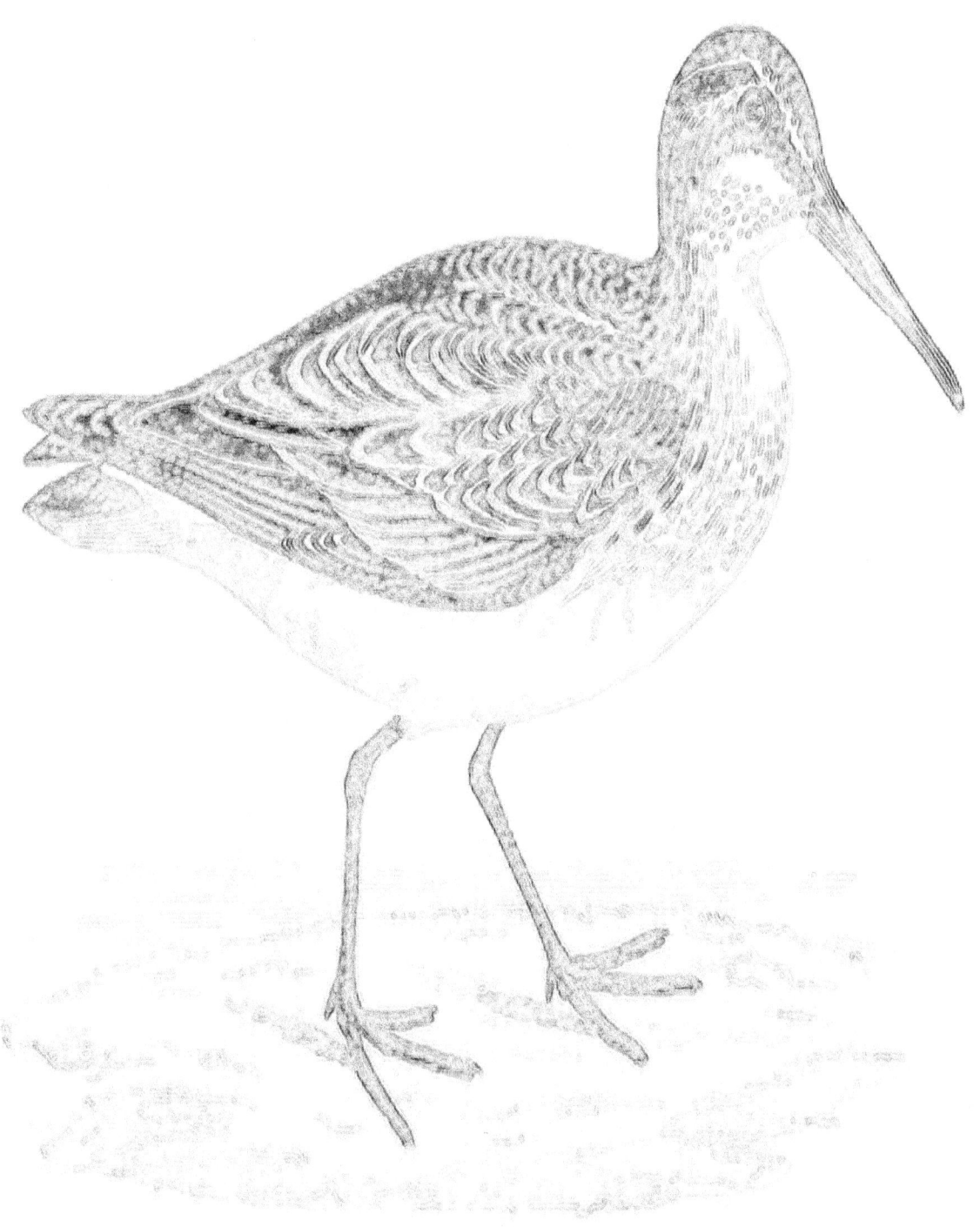

BROWN SNIPE

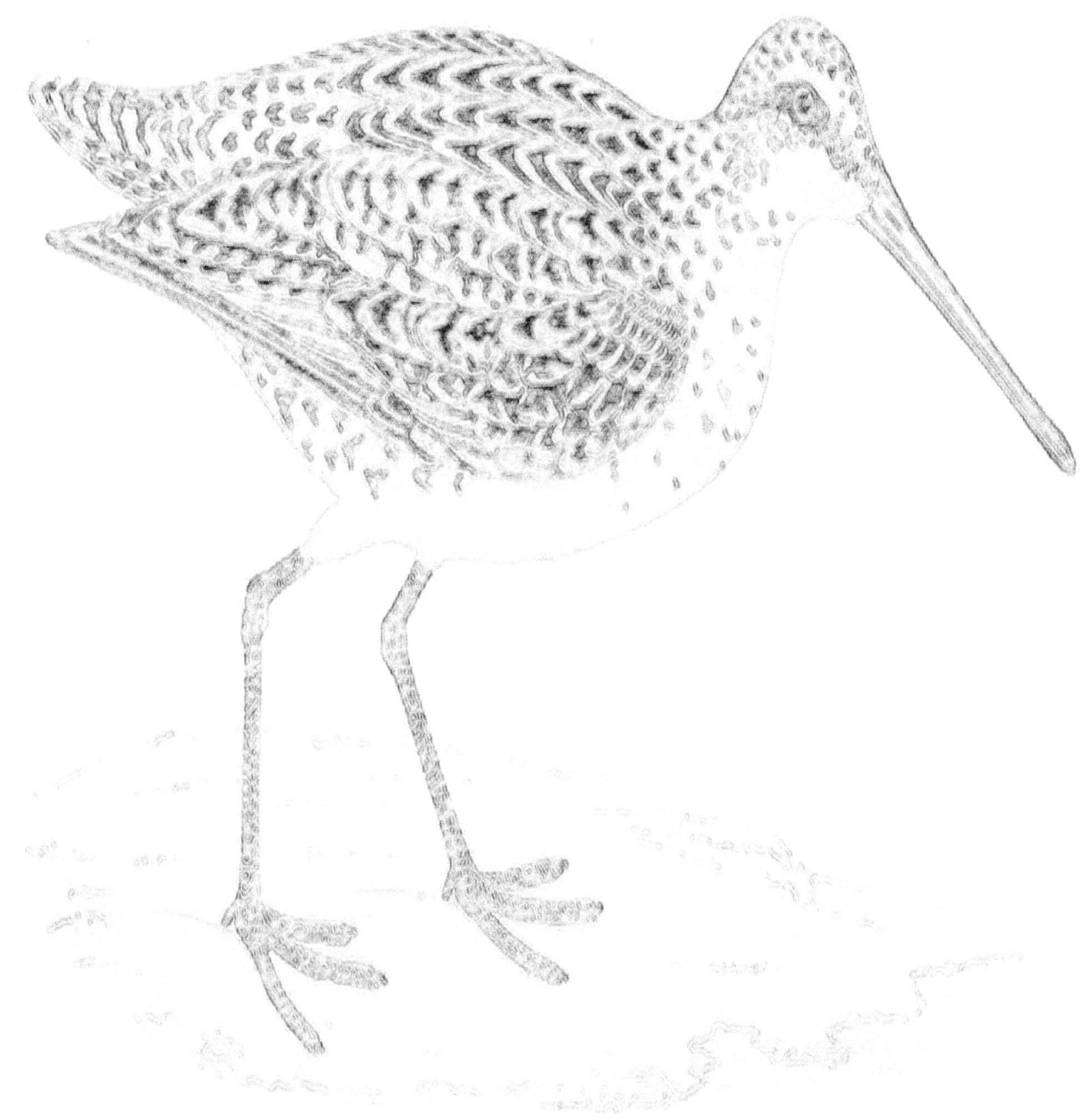

BUFF-BACKED HERON

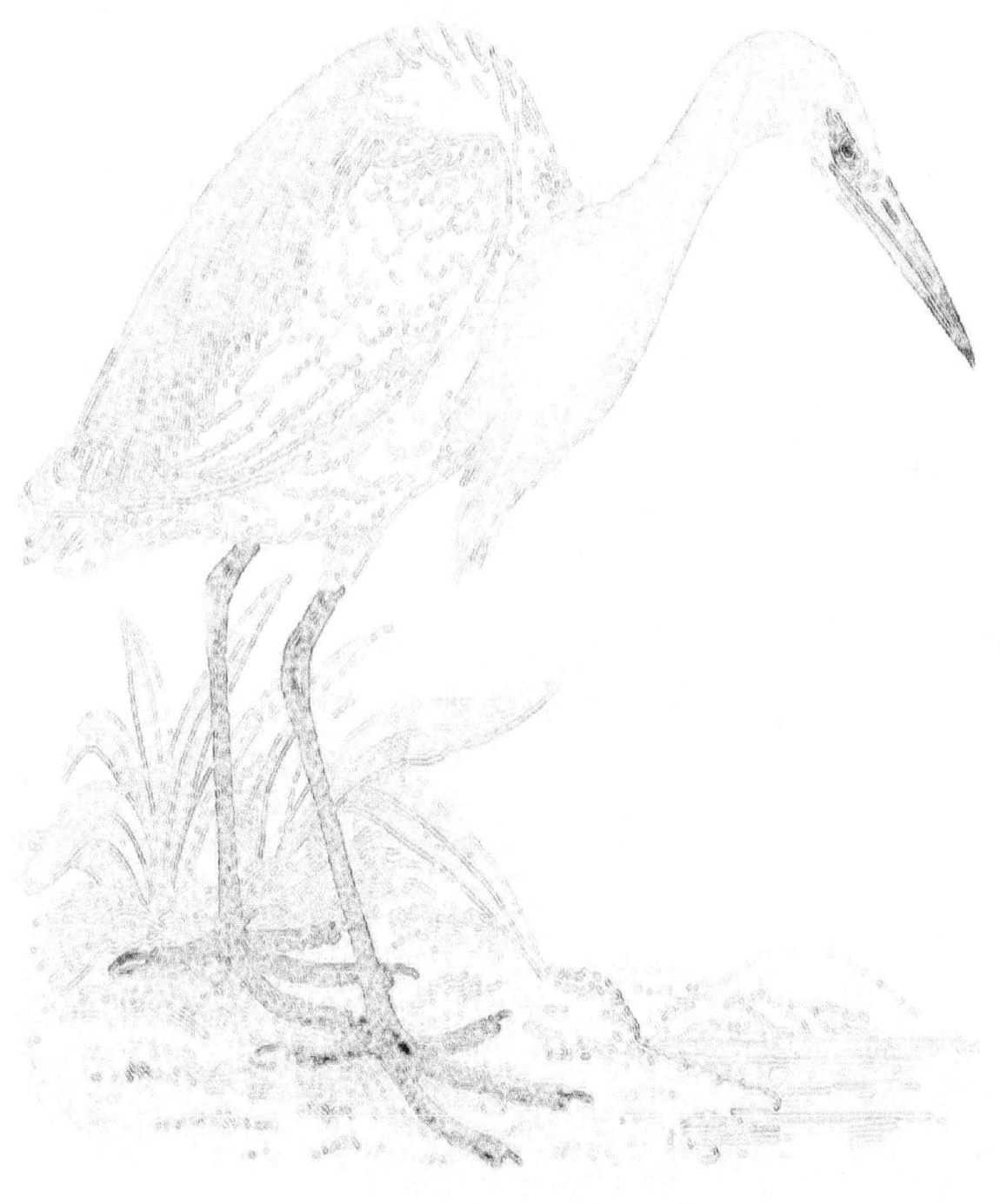

BULLFINCH

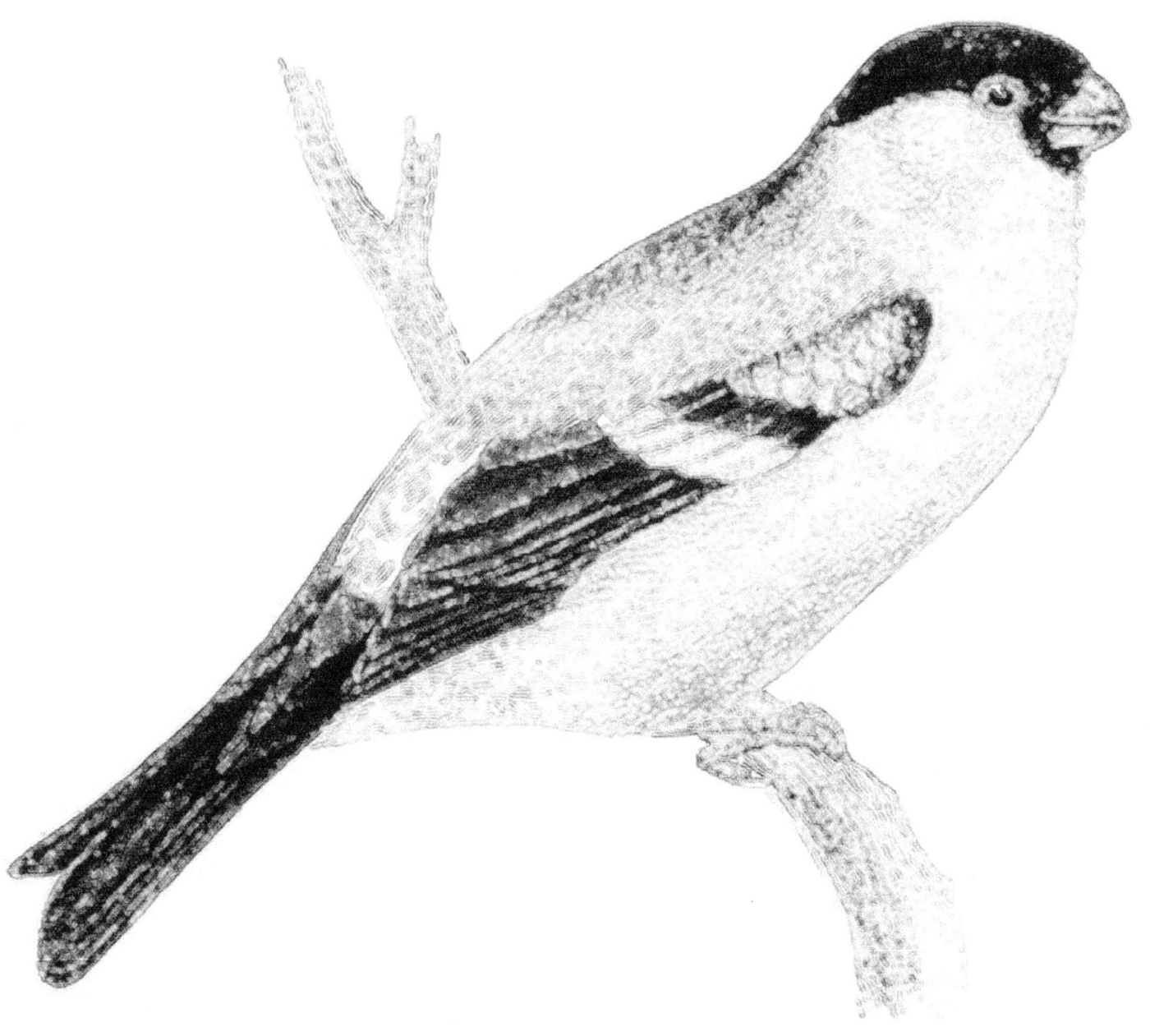

CHAFFINCH

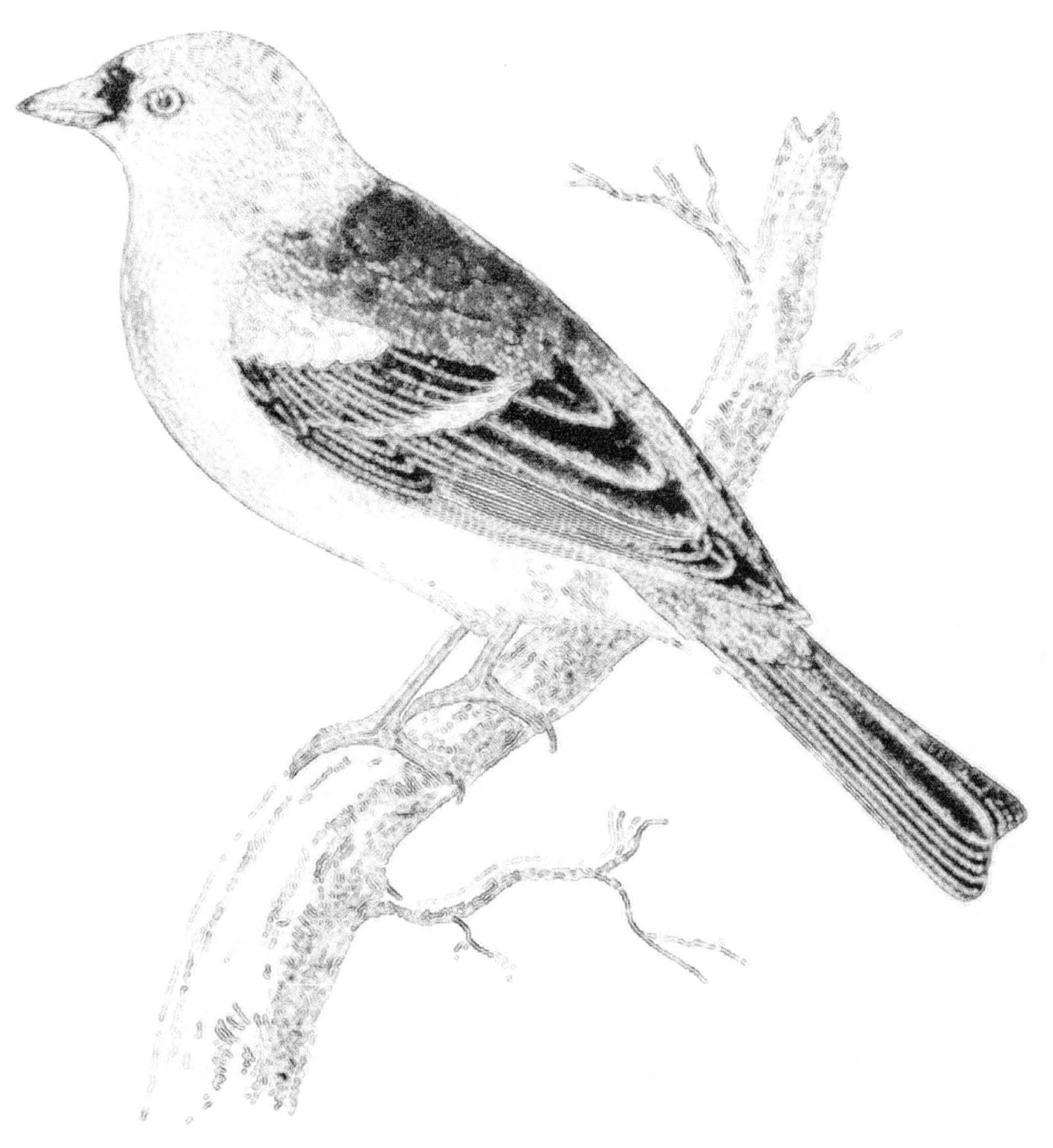

CIRL BUNTING

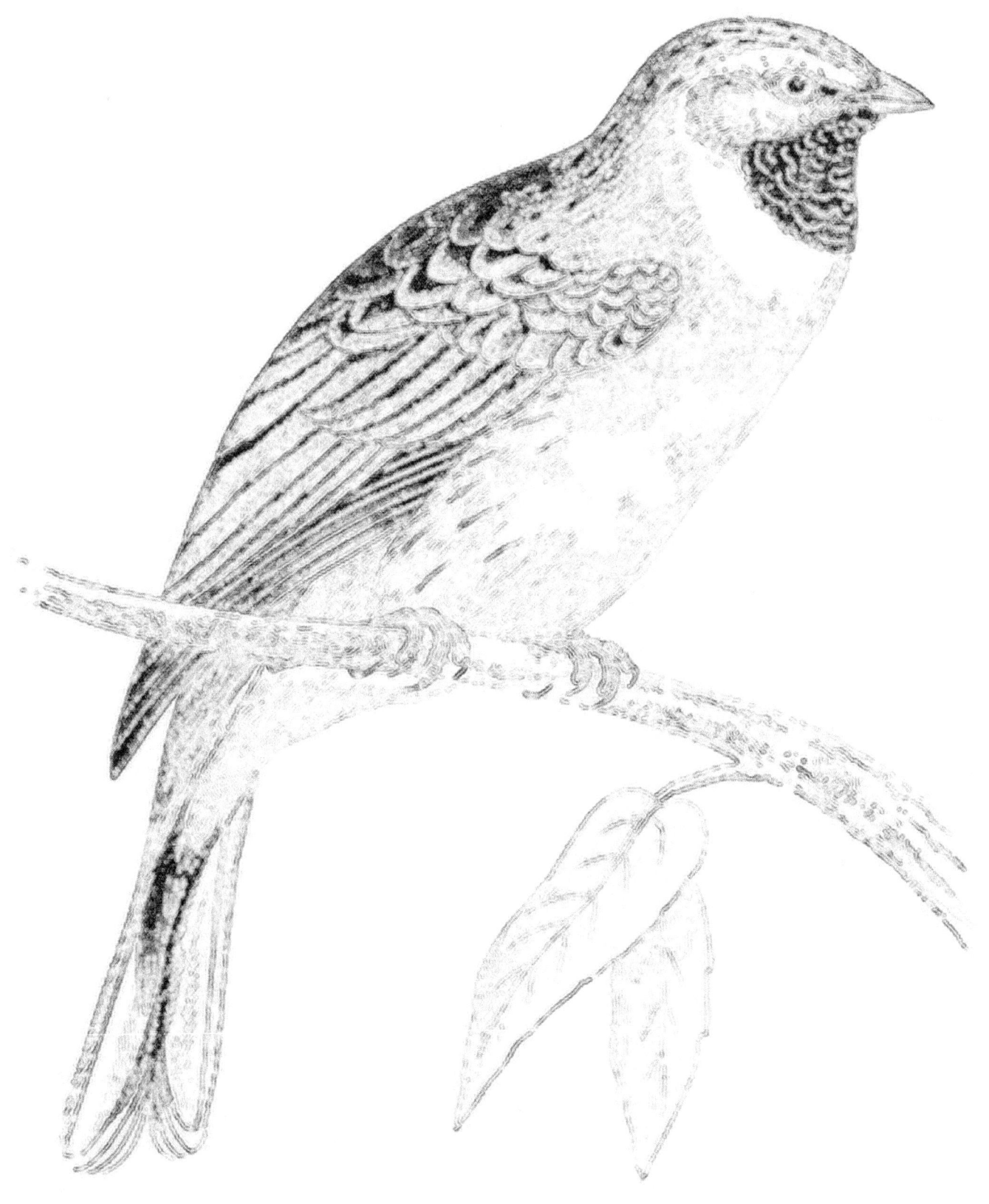

COURSER

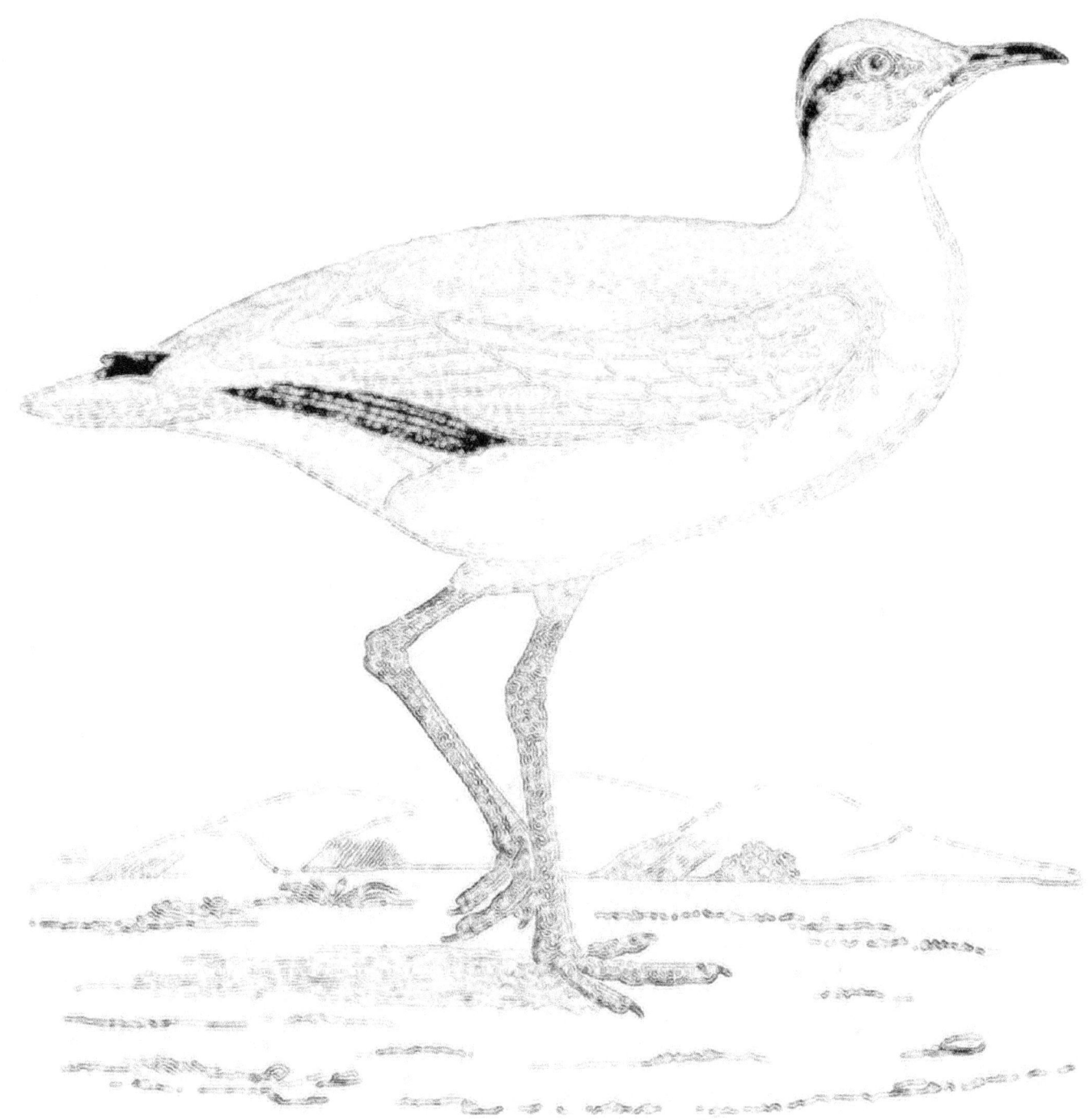

CRANE

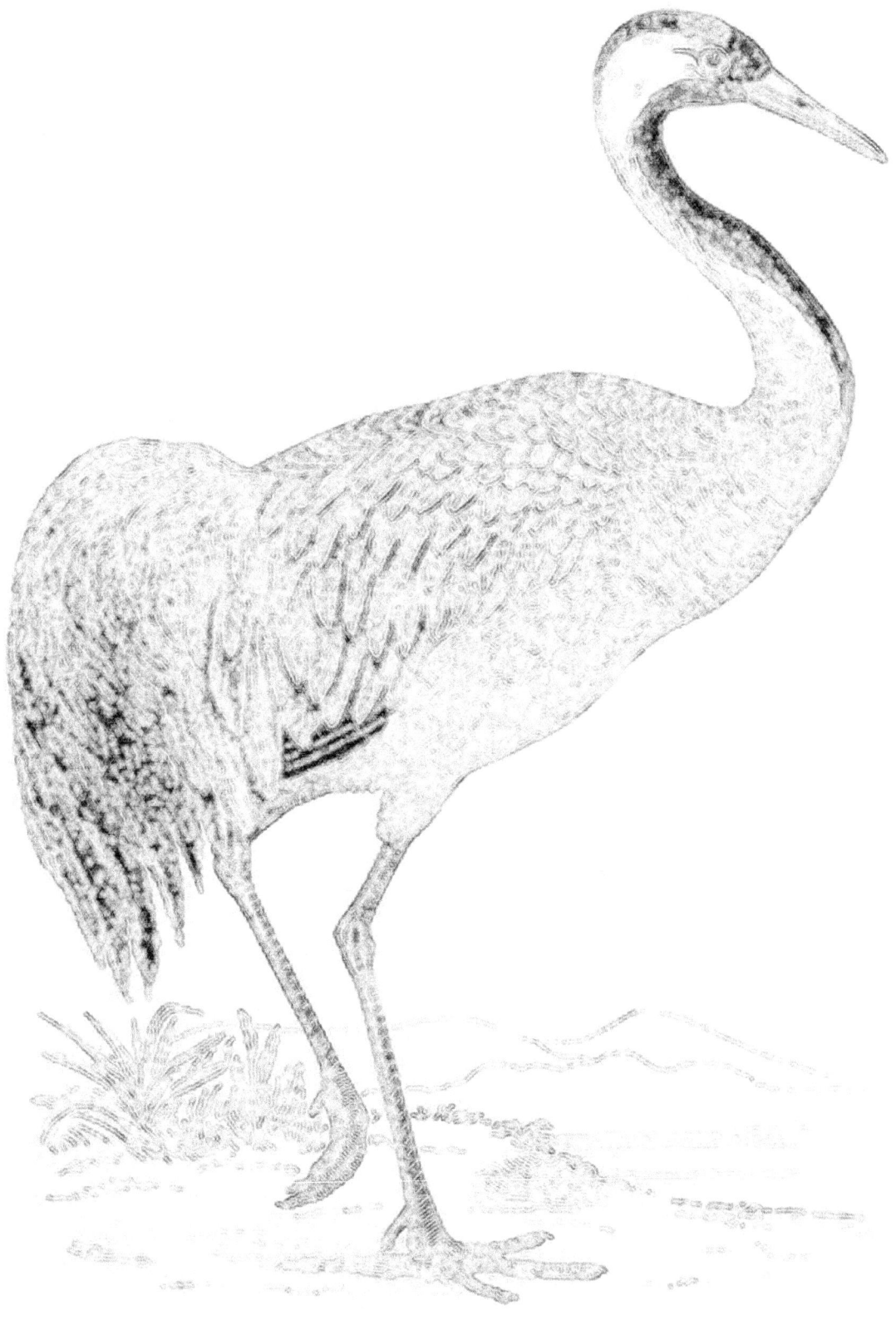

CREEPER

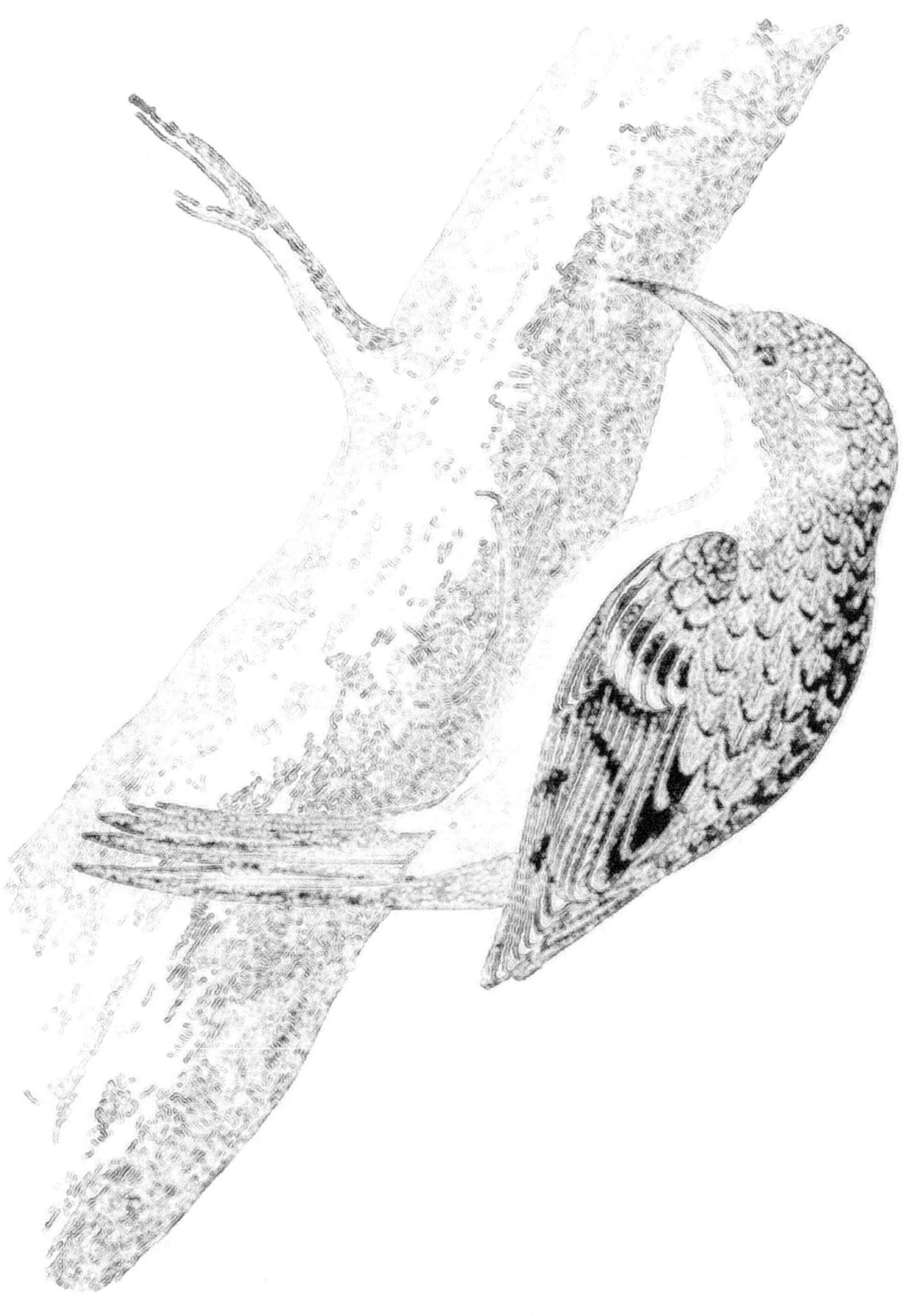

CURLEW SANDPIPER

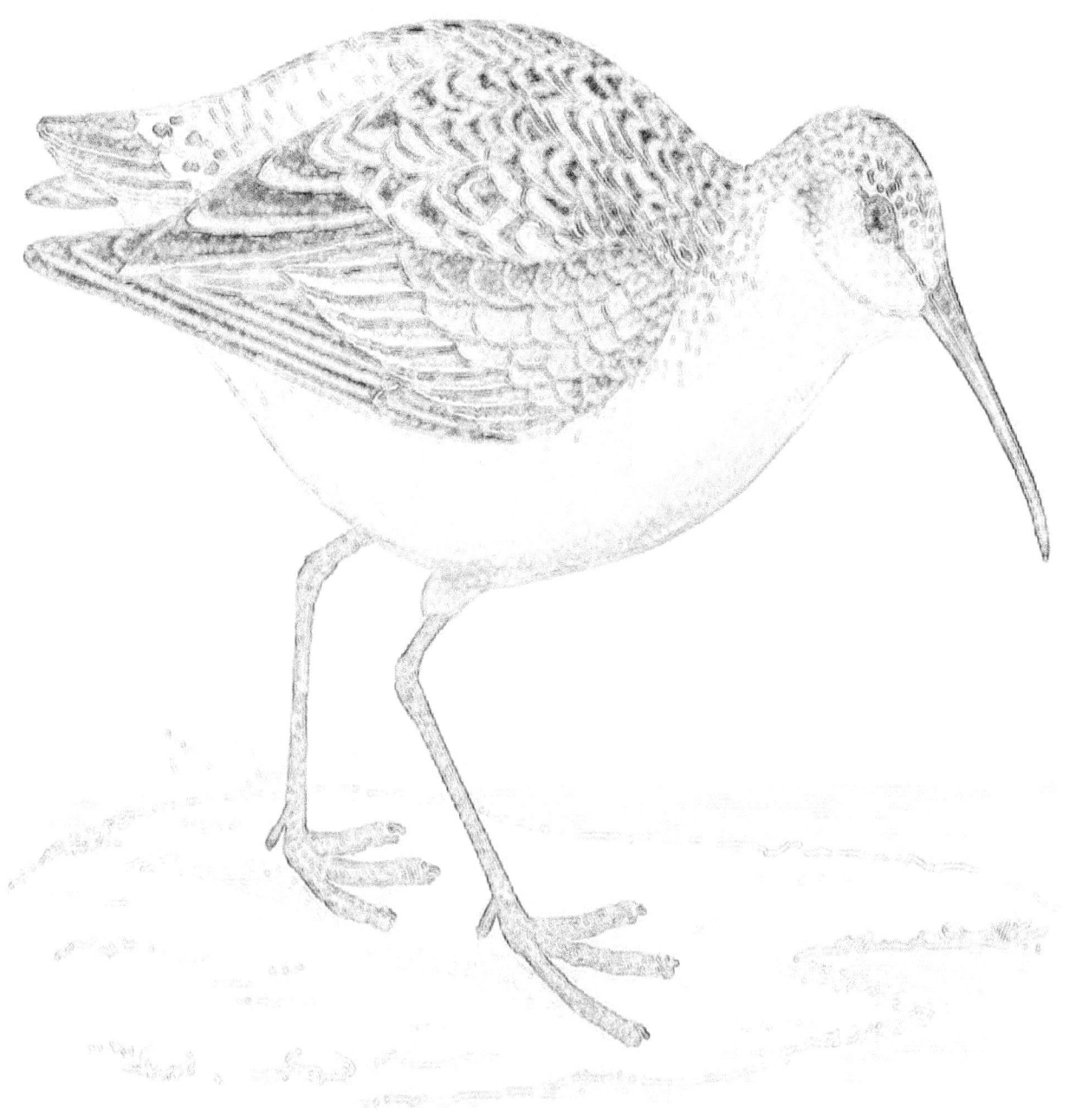

CURLEW

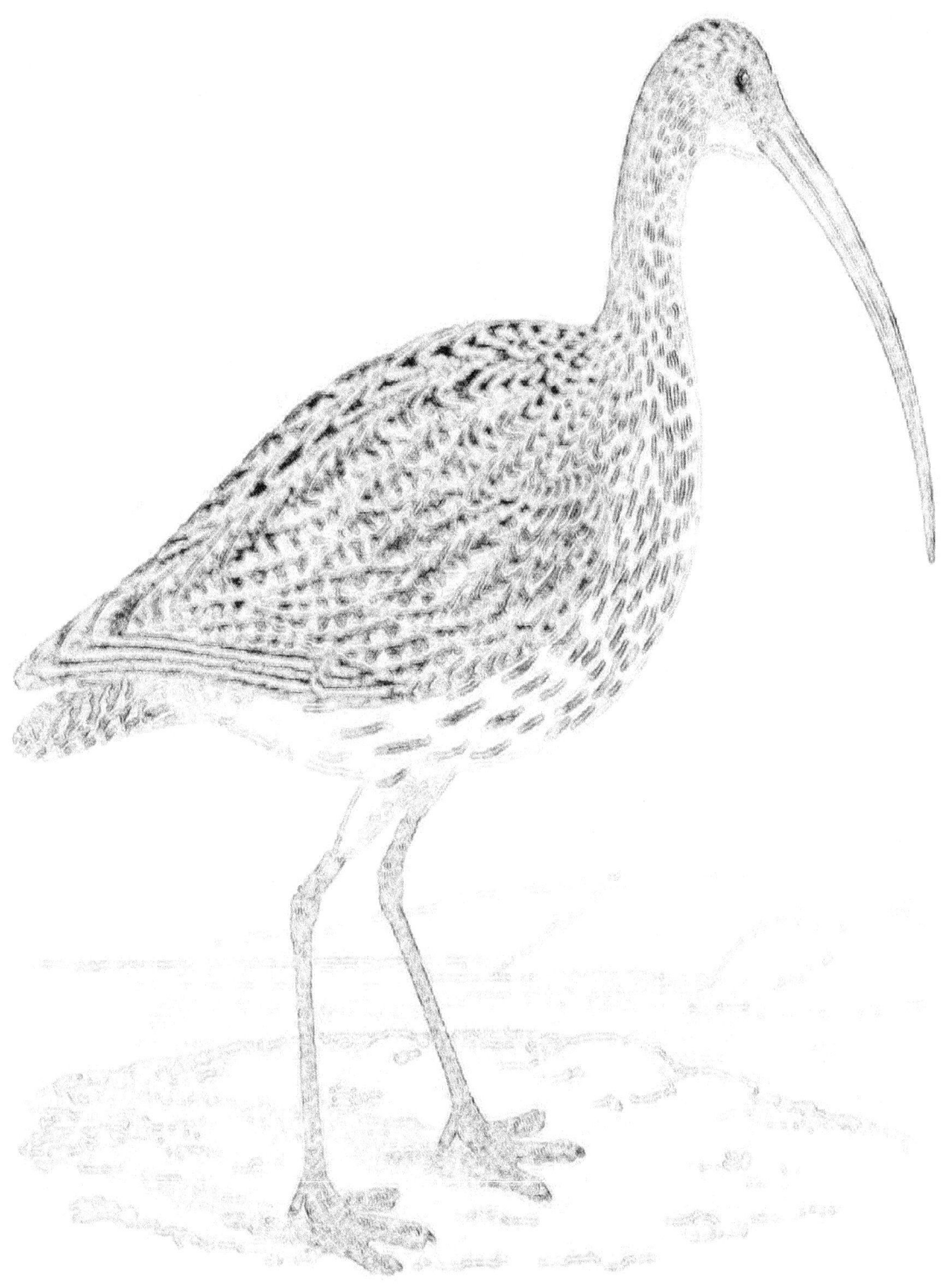

DARTFORD WARBLER

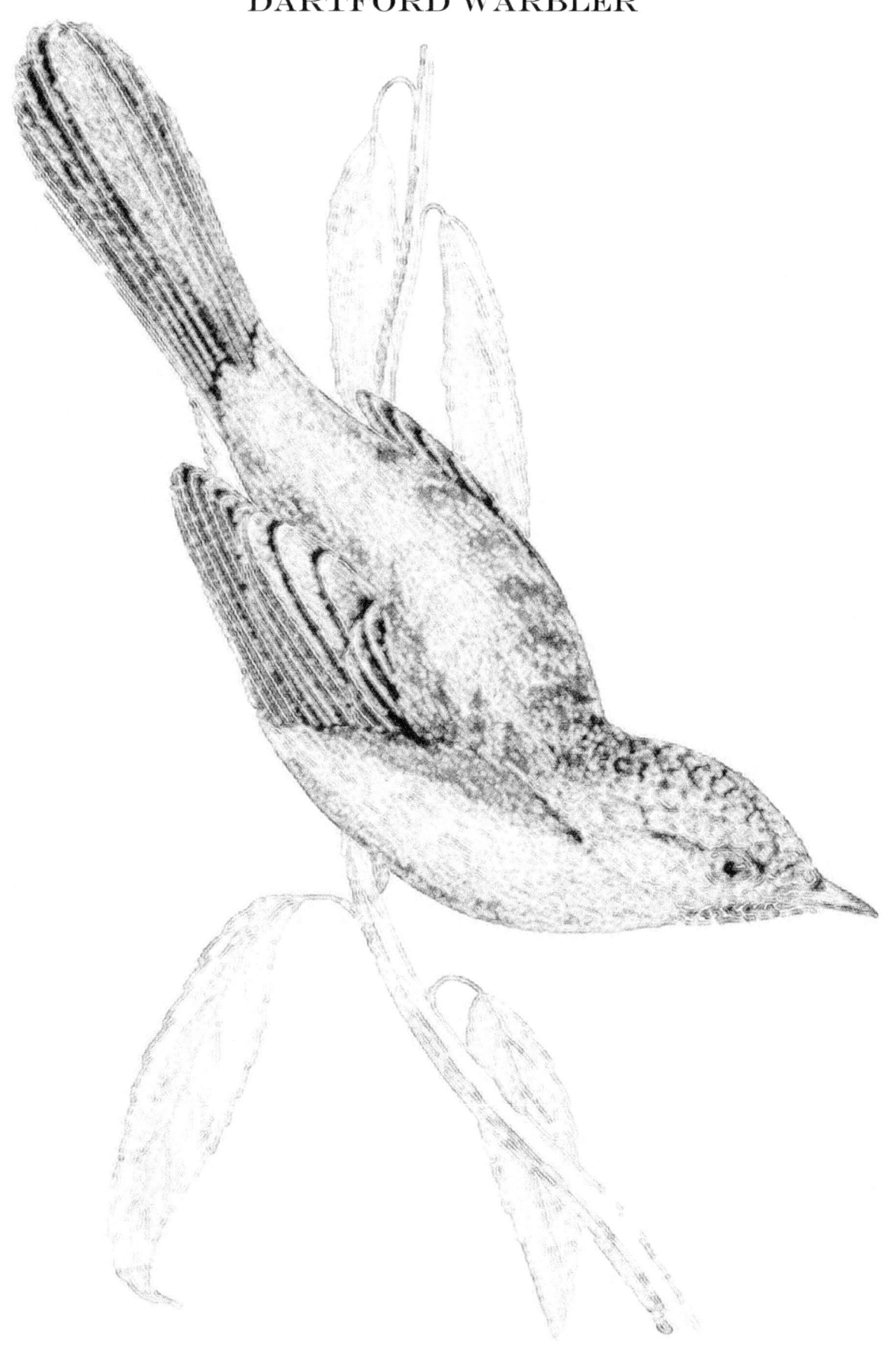

DESERT WHEATEAR

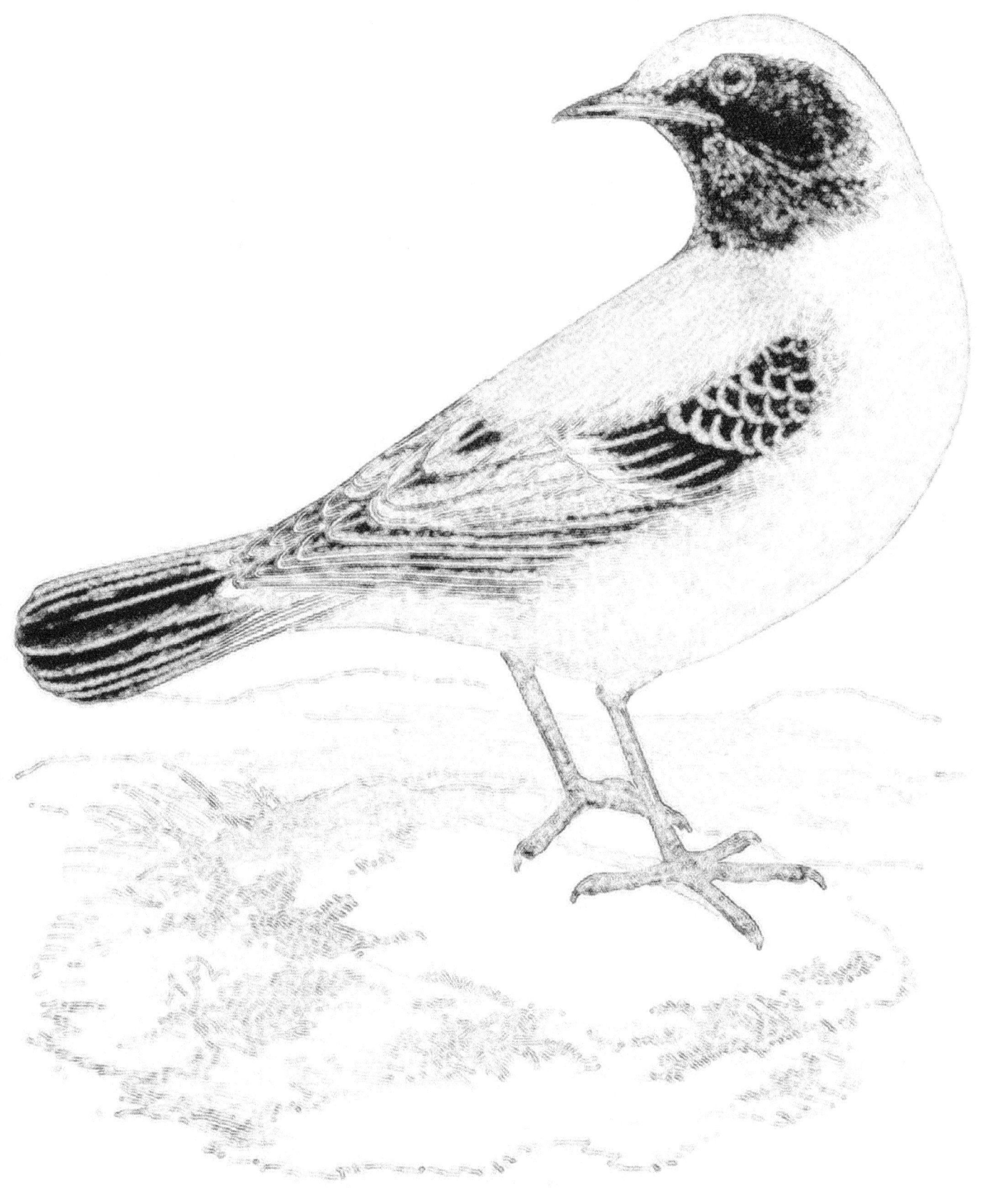

DOTTEREL

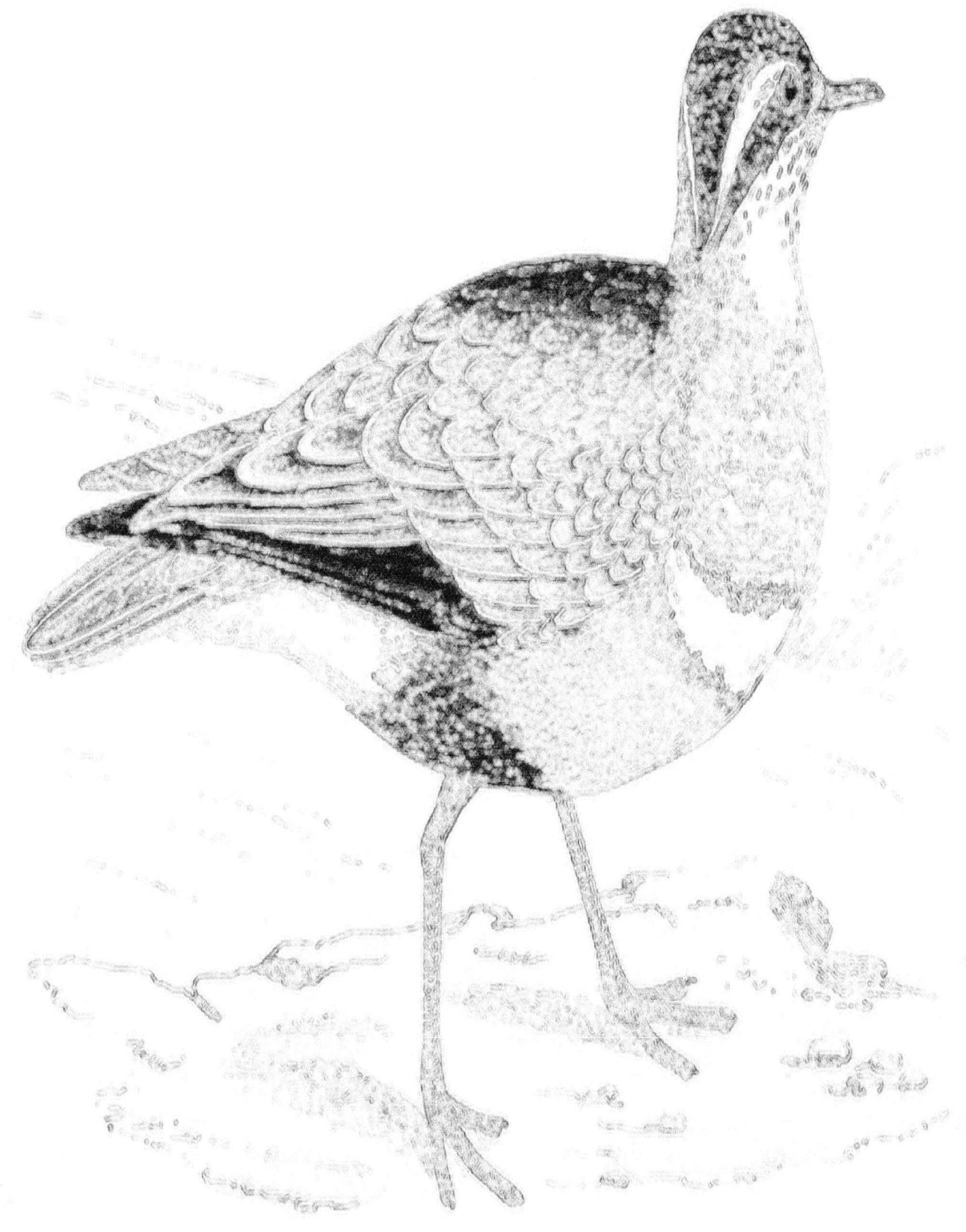

DUNLIN

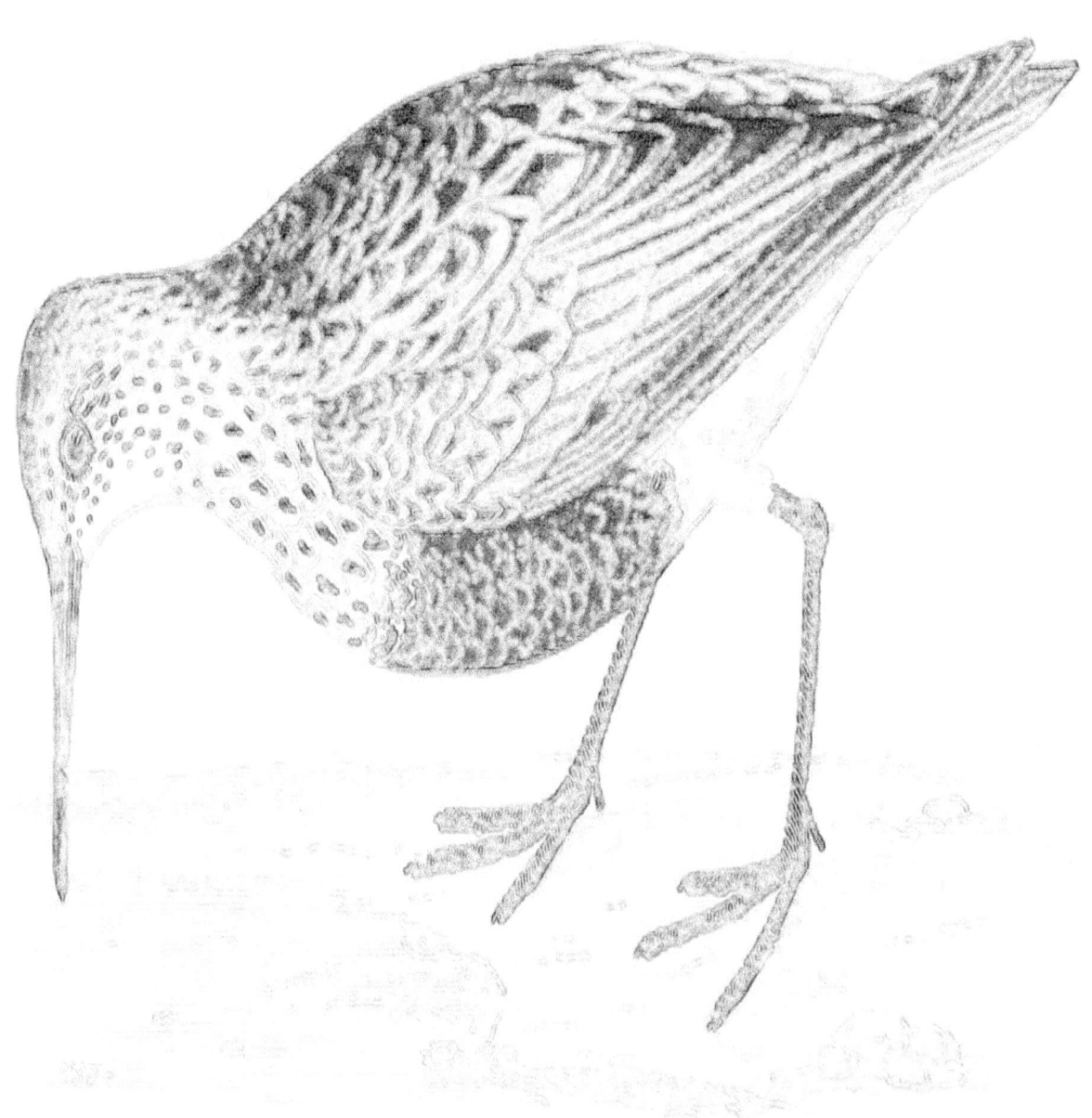

www.ingramcontent.com/pod-product-compliance
Lightning Source LLC
Chambersburg PA
CBHW080600190526
45169CB00007B/2835